GEORGIOS TERLAKIS

SOUNIO
LAURIO & THORIKOS

EDITIONS

TOUBI'S
ΕΚΔΟΣΕΙΣ
ATHENS 2004

© Copyright 2004   MICHAEL TOUBIS PUBLICATIONS S.A.
Nisiza Karela, Koropi, Attiki.
Telephone: +30 210 6029974, Fax: +30 210 6646856
Web Site: http://www.toubis.gr

ISBN: 960-540-521-0

Engraving of Sounio by. J.B. Lechevalier.

"I was returning to get to know Attica,

that is what I thought;

but I was returning to get to know my soul;

in the trees, in the mountains, in the solitude I sought

to find and to know my soul - all was in vain;

my heart did not pulse, an indisputable sign

that I was not to find what I sought.

One day, only, just one noon, I thought I found it.

I had gone alone to Sounio; the sun was burning and summer

had come, the wounded pines were bleeding resin and the air

was redolent with its aroma; a cicada came and sat

on my shoulder and for some time we walked together;

all of me smelled of pine, I had become one; and suddenly,

as I walked out of the grove of pine trees, I saw the white

columns of the Temple of Poseidon and in between them,

the glittering, dark blue, the blessed sea. My knees buckled,

I came to a standstill. "This is Beauty", I thought,

"this is wingless Nike, the apex of joy

- man cannot reach anything higher".

This is Greece..."

Nikos Kazantzakis
(excerpt from *Report to Greco*)

CONTENTS

MAP OF LAUREOTIKI

SOUNIO

The "sacred promontory" of Sounio, as Homer called it in his Odyssey, is situated on the south east edge of the peninsula of Attica, 67 kilometres from Athens. On the highest point of this isolated cape, at a height of 70 metres from the sea, are the ruins of the Temple of Poseidon; the "Cavo Kolones", as sailors call them. To the east, one can see Makronessos and further away, one can see the nearest of the Cycladic Islands, Kea, also known as Tzia. To the south are the blue waters of the Aegean and the islet of Aghios Giorgos, while to the west is the small island, Patroclus. On clear days, one can see Milos, Hydra and the Peloponnese. The sea, the picturesque shores and the small islands just across, charm all visitors who, enraptured with the view at sunset, allow their imaginations to take them centuries back in time.

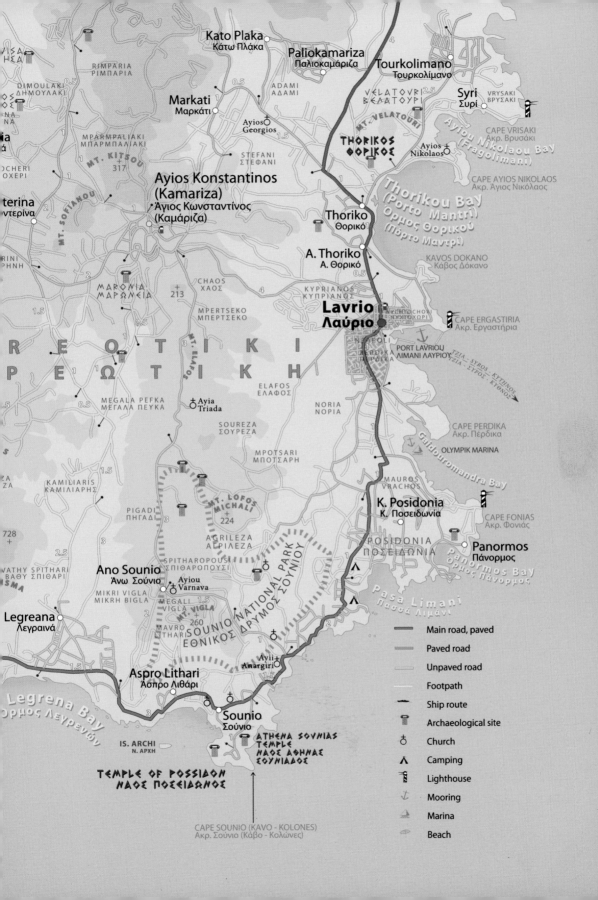

THE TEMPLE
OF
POSEIDON

WORSHIP

The outdoor worship that took place at Sounio was not the simple worship of one god, as one could naturally - but mistakenly - infer from the name of the temple. The worship that took place there was complex and it is worth examining through the historical, social and mythological context in which it developed.

Through the examination of findings which date back mainly from the 8th century to the 6th century BC (swords, plaque of a ship with hoplites, arrows etc), one can see that worship at Sounio before the temple was built was of a military nature, male oriented and that the naval element was dominant. This, taken into account firstly with the fact that there is no evidence that any Olympian gods were worshipped on the site before the temple was built and secondly, Homer's reference to the fact that the hero Phrontes was buried on this site, would lead us to the conclusion that in those early years the cult of the hero Phrontes dominated in the area. The worship of this Laconian hero that took place in Sounio encompassed both his naval and his earthly nature - two qualities which are characteristic of the pre-Doric Laconic deities, the Dioscuri.

The Dioscuri were the twin warrior gods, Castor and Pollux. The myths surrounding them say that Zeus seduced their mother, Leda, by taking the shape of a swan. From this union, Leda bore two eggs. Castor and Pollux emerged from the one egg, while, Helen, later to become notorious in the Trojan War, emerged from the other. The two brothers were bound by a strong filial love. Their father, Zeus, granted them immortality and they lived alternately on Olympus and in Hades. The Dioscuri symbolise the hope of mortals for resurrection as they lived, so to speak, both in the underworld and on the earth. The Dioscuri were also considered the protectors and saviours of sailors.

Many ancient writers such as Homer, Dionysus of Halicarnassus, Theocritus, Herodotus, Pausanias and others, refer to the Dioscuri, while Lucian wrote that their divine powers were devoted to the service of Poseidon. Worship of the Dioscuri was widespread all over Greece, but was most notable in Attica.

At the end of the 7th century BC, the first four marble Kouroi, which sailors gazed at as they travelled by, were placed in Sounio; this marked the beginning of a new phase of outdoor worship. The purpose of the Kouroi (which were also to be found throughout the rest of Greece) was to be used either as votive statues or as markers for graves. These Kouroi, as votive offerings

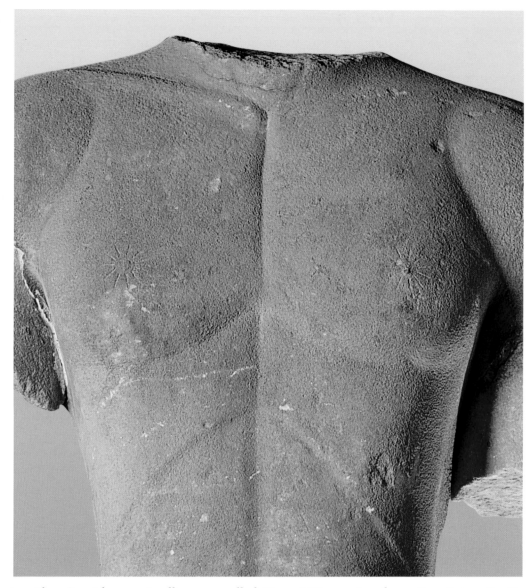

to either Poseidon or Apollo, were called Kouroi Dioscuri and with their presence, sailors endeavoured to propitiate Poseidon or Apollo when they were in danger from him as he was associated with the death of Phrontes, as well as the disappearance of many sailors.

In 480 BC the Persians wiped out every trace of worship (the poros stone temple, the Kouroi, altars). When the great marble Temple of Poseidon, (444 - 440 BC) was constructed, the temple phase of this sacred site began with the worship of two Olympian gods; the god of the sea, Poseidon, and Athena Sounias. Naturally, the worship of Poseidon predominated.

Torso of a larger than life size Kouros from 600 BC exchibited at the National Archaeological Museum. The stars on the nipples, a symbol of the Dioscuri, can be discerned.

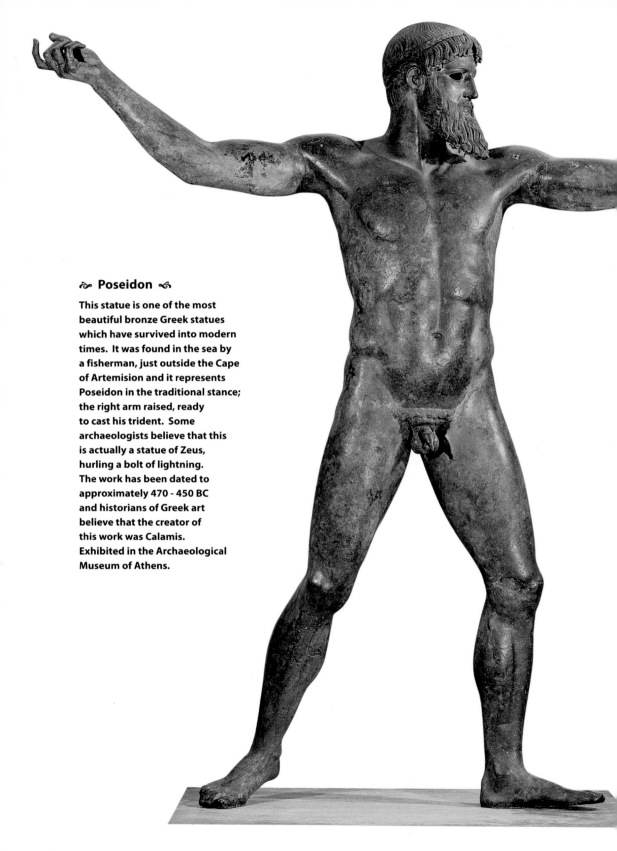

❧ Poseidon ❧

This statue is one of the most beautiful bronze Greek statues which have survived into modern times. It was found in the sea by a fisherman, just outside the Cape of Artemision and it represents Poseidon in the traditional stance; the right arm raised, ready to cast his trident. Some archaeologists believe that this is actually a statue of Zeus, hurling a bolt of lightning. The work has been dated to approximately 470 - 450 BC and historians of Greek art believe that the creator of this work was Calamis. Exhibited in the Archaeological Museum of Athens.

POSEIDON

According to Hesiod's *Theogony*, Cronus and Rhea had three sons and three daughters: Zeus, Poseidon, Hades, Hera, Demeter and Hestia. In the *Iliad*, Poseidon is referred to as one of the most respected of the Olympian gods. As the terrible god of the sea, his symbol was the trident. With it he agitated the sea so that ships would sink but it was also with his trident that he would calm the waves and bring serenity to troubled waters. He must have initially been a *chthonic* (of the netherworld, or of the earth) god as can be seen by the etymology of his name and from the adjectives that Homer used to describe him which associated him with the earth (e.g. Poseidon *gaieochus* = he who carries the Earth). It was believed that he lived in the bowels of the Earth and that he controlled rivers and springs. Hesiod wrote that it was Poseidon who kept the Titans prisoner in Tartarus, the lowest reaches of the underworld.

Later, the Ionians associated him with the sea. Calm seas and stormy ones were ascribed to the god's good graces or to his rage and anger. In older times, when the gods were worshipped in the incarnation of wild animals, Poseidon was worshipped as a horse. In Thessaly, it was believed that the god hit his trident against a rock and the first horse was thus created. In Arcadia, he was given the name Poseidon the "Ippios" (from the ancient Greek word *hippos* = horse). In mythology, the winged horse Pegasus was thought to be the offspring of Poseidon and Medusa. Apart from horses, Poseidon was also associated with bulls. In reading the ancient myths, it becomes clear that he was considered responsible for a series of geological phenomena such as earthquakes and avalanches. This can be seen by his cognomens: *Gaies Kiniter* (the Earth Mover), *Gaieochus* (the Earth Carrier), *Seisichthon* (He who Shakes the Earth), *Damsichton* (the Earth Tamer).

Based on these qualities, it was only natural that the ancients evoked his protection to ensure the stability of the ground and, by extension, the security of their homes. He was worshipped as the *Edraeus* (the Foundation), *Themeliouchos* (the Underpinner) and the *Teichopoeos* (the Wall-maker). It was also believed that he was responsible for rivers and lakes, but this is a power that was ascribed to him later and in this incarnation he was worshipped as the *Krenaeus* (from the word for spring and the *Epilemnios* (from the word for lake).

Silver drachma depicting Poseidon, 306-283 BC. Nautical Museum of the Aegean.

His association with the liquid element was the last quality to be ascribed to the god. He was worshipped as *Alius, Thalassomedon, Isthmius* and *Porthmius* (all of these words have to do with the sea; aquatic, oceanic, maritime, marine) . From reading Mycenaean texts, it appears that before the Olympian phase of the twelve gods, the worship of Poseidon competed neck to neck with that of Zeus. In the Olympian religion of the twelve gods, when the world was being divided up, Poseidon was allotted responsibility for the sea. All the myths which have to do with Poseidon's conflicts with other gods over favoured cities were born from the need to explain the decline of his cult in these areas.

This is why he was ascribed an irascible and vindictive temperament which, on the one hand justified the fact that he lost the areas he sought influence over, but on the other hand maintained the full gravity of his religious stature in the minds of the people.

ATHENA

Athena was born from the union of Zeus and Metis, daughter of Oceanus and Tethys. Uranus and Gaea told Zeus that Metis would bear him a daughter who would take after her father in courage and brains and a son who would become smarter than Zeus and might threaten his supremacy when he reached adulthood. Fearing this prophecy, Zeus swallowed Metis in order to avoid this eventuality. When the time came for Athena to be born, Zeus ordered Hephaestus to open his head with a blow of an axe. To the consternation of all, the goddess sprang full-grown and armoured from the head of Zeus. The idiosyncratic manner of her birth demonstrates her close relationship to Zeus and this was a feature of her cult as well.

Athena was the goddess of Wisdom. Clever and resourceful and with a complex make up, she stood by heroes and philosophers and was at the fore in developing the arts of peacetime. Athena *"Promachus"* protected the Greeks in their military expeditions by giving them advice and encouragement as well as with her active involvement in their struggles. She helped the demi-gods such as Hercules and she gave her grace to great heroes, famous for their razor sharp minds, such as Odysseus. Athena *"Soteira"* did whatever she could to avoid gratuitous bloodshed in battle and she tried to save those that she protected from death. She always tried to end wars with the least possible loss of human life. Athena *"Ergane"* first taught the arts to the Cyclops and thence to

*Coin depicting
the head of Athena.*

humans. In myths, she is described as the agent of civilisation as it was she, together with Hephaestus, who taught humanity how to make beautiful things. It was she who first taught people the art of the loom and the first embroideries and woven fabrics are ascribed to her.

Relief carving of the goddes Athena, known as the "thinking Athena". The goddess is wearing a Doric peplos (dress) tied at the waist and a helmet and she is barefoot. 460 BC. Athens, Acropolis Museum.

THE CONFLICT BETWEEN ATHENA AND POSEIDON

Myth would have it that at one time Poseidon and Athena argued over who would reign supreme in Attica. In the end, they agreed that each would offer the inhabitants a gift and the winner would be the one who had offered the most valuable gift according to the verdict of the other gods. Poseidon struck the hill on which the Acropolis was built with his trident and water gushed out. Another version of the myth states that it was the first horse which came out. Athena, in her turn, struck the rock with her spear and the first olive tree sprouted up. The gods gave Athena the prize and the city was thus named after her. A similar myth states that Cecrops, the king of the city, which was then called Cecropia, was the judge in this contest. Pausanias wrote that the western pediment of the Parthenon had a representation of the dispute between Poseidon and Athena. Athena became the goddess protector of the city and her cult was founded on the sacred rock of the Acropolis. The temple devoted to her, the Parthenon, was the most important temple in the city throughout antiquity and a masterpiece of classical Greek architecture. The cult of Poseidon, on the other hand, was limited to a temple near the spot where his trident struck, which, in the 5th century BC, was housed, along with other small temples in the Erechtheum, next to the Parthenon. The Athenians, naturally, were not boorish enough to forget the god of the sea as Athens was mainly a maritime state. They quickly understood that Poseidon would be unhappy if there seemed to

The conflict between Athena and Poseidon depicted on a black figure ware attic amphora made by the potter Amasios (6th century BC).

be any inequality in the honours that were paid him. Therefore, they built a majestic temple on Cape Sounio, at the spot where, in the past, both Athena and Poseidon had been worshipped. In this way, they hoped to propitiate the god who wielded the terrible trident.

According, therefore, to one theory, the development of religious worship on Sounio began with the hero Phrontes where his grave stood, then went on to the pre-Olympian worship of the Dioscuri and ended up with the worship of two Olympian gods: Poseidon and Athena. Poseidon had the senior position in Sounio and he was also considered to have qualities which belonged to the other gods. Furthermore, various inscriptions at Sounio testify to the fact that other gods were also worshipped there; some of the inscribed names found are Zeus Sounios, Apollo, Zeus Melichios, Asclepius and others.

THESEUS - MINOTAUR

Sounio is referred to in archaeology as the cape from which Aegeus flung himself into the sea. According to the myth, when Aegeus was the king of Athens, a curse loomed over the land. The inhabitants of Athens had killed Androgeus, the son of Minos. Minos compelled the Athenians to send seven youths and seven maidens to the Minotaur for nine years. The third time that this was to happen, Theseus, son of Aegeus, insisted on being included in this group.

The ship which was to carry the group to Crete had two sets of sails; one white and one black. On leaving for Crete the ship used its black sails which Theseus promised to replace with the white on his return as a sign that he had managed to kill the Minotaur. Theseus duly defeated him and set off for Athens carrying on his ship not only the youths he had saved, but also Ariadne, Minos' daughter with whom he had fallen in love. However, he had forgotten to change the sails of his ship. Thus, Aegeus, who was impatiently awaiting his son's return in Sounio, saw the black sails and, in despair, fell into the sea where he drowned. Since then, this sea has been called the Aegean.

Theseus killing the Minotaur (black figure ware amphora, Paris, Louvre).

HISTORY

The first historical source to mention Sounio is the Odyssey: *"When we got to Sunium, which is the point of Athens..."* (Odyssey Book III).

This line comes from Nestor's, the king of Pylos and the oldest of the rulers who had taken part in the Trojan War, recounting of his wanderings after the war to Odysseus' son, Telemachus.

Homer's verse tells of ancient worship in Sounio in the early Hellenic years. Homer also informs us that it was in Sounio that Phrontes Onetorides, the steersman of Menelaus' ship, was buried after he was killed by Apollo on the return journey of the

Achaeans after the Trojan war. In the same tradition, Pausanias explained why the ancient name of Makronessos was the isle of Helen. It seems that Helen waited on this island for her husband Menelaus to return from burying Prhrontes in Sounio.

In the Archaic period (7th - 6th century BC), the Athenians recognised Sounion's strategic position and the importance of building up the defences of the fortress which guarded the entry of ships in to the Saronic Gulf. They began construction of a strong wall with polygonal blocks on the northern and western sides.

*Painting of
the Temple of Poseidon.*

It was around 600 BC that the monumental marble Kouroi - those larger than life-size youths, with the even gaze and the almost imperceptible smile - must have been placed there.

At the beginning of the 5th century, construction began on the first porous rock temple dedicated to Poseidon. However, before it was finished, it was destroyed by the Persians in 480 BC. Later, after the triumphant victory of Salamis, Herodotus informs us that the Athenians made sacrifices in Sounio in honour of the sea god, Poseidon.

The "laureotic glauce".

Nearby Laurio played an important role in the victory, as its mines were fully exploited following a proposal by Themistocles. The end of the war with the Persians marked the beginning of Athenian supremacy. Commerce, as well as other areas of life flourished and the *"laureotic glauces"* became a strong currency all over the Hellenic world. Sounio also played a significant role in the Peloponnesian War due to its strategic position.

The historian of this war, Thucydides, wrote that in the spring of 413 BC, the king of Sparta, Ages, conquered Deceleia which was only 20 kilometres away from Athens. From Deceleia, the Spartans controlled the neighbouring region and stopped supplies from Euboea via Oropos reaching Athens. The Athenians, in order to ensure that their ships carrying foodstuffs reached the city, strengthened the fortifications of Sounio by supporting the old polygonic wall with a new one in which marble plinths were also placed.

The next military adventure that Sounio was involved in was the Chraemonideios War (266-262 BC) and immediately afterwards (263 - 229 BC) it was occupied by the Macedonians. In 263 BC, as Pausanias wrote, the fortress, despite furious resistance on the part of the Athenians, was conquered by Antigonus Gonatas, king of Macedon. Athens once again took over the fort in 229 BC when Aratos, unable to dislodge the Macedonians by force of arms, bribed the castellan, Diogenes, with 150 talants.

At the end of the 2nd century BC, approximately 1,000 slaves from the Laurio mines took over the fortress after the widespread slave uprisings which began in Sicily.

The Laurio mines closed in the 2nd century BC. The complete absence of any reference to Sounio in the historical documents of the following years seems to indicate the sudden decline of the site both as a strategic site and as a place of worship.

HISTORICAL FRAMEWORK

For many centuries, it was believed that the temple built on the rocky crags of Sounio was one dedicated to the goddess Athena. This misconception began with the traveller and geographer Pausanias in the 2nd century AD. Pausanias, in his book "Attica", referred to Sounio, writing that it had one temple only, that of Athena Sounias:

"...and the Temple of Athena Sounias on the tip of the extremity".

It seems that a copier of the Pausanias' manuscripts omitted some phrase from his text or that Pausanias' information on the region was wrong. Reading the text, one understands that he never visited the site, but rather wrote his description based on his viewing from a passing ship. Since then and for 18 eighteen centuries, all references to Sounio repeated and therefore reinforced the mistake in speaking of it as a Temple to Athena.

Pausanias made one more reference to Sounio in a well known description which, while not mistaken, is exaggerated for the sake of romance. In describing the superb statue of Athena Promachus on the Acropolis (in Athens), he wrote that the tip of her spear was visible to those sailing by Cape Sounio.

Another writer from Roman times, Vitruvius, referred to

"Plato and his students at Sounio".
Anacharsis, 1798.

the temple of Athena Sounias and, despite the fact that his description in no wise describes the Temple of Poseidon, no one commented on it. Thus, for centuries, no one imagined that there were two sanctuaries on Sounio; that the temple at the top of the cliff was dedicated to the mighty god of the sea and that the sanctuary of Athena was on a small hill north east of Poseidon's temple.

Until the 17th century, there were no references made to the temples of Sounio. No one knows when and how the temple of Poseidon was destroyed. Tradition has it that in the black years of the Ottoman Empire, the few inhabitants of the nearby villages believed that the marble columns of the temple were the ruins of some palace. They dug and searched to find hidden

treasure and thus destroyed what was left.

De Vega in 1537 was the first of the modern travellers to mention the temple and he wrote that there were eighteen surviving columns; Trasfeldt in 1674 referred to seventeen, while Wheler in 1676 referred to nine columns on the southern side (the number still extant today) and five on the northern side (the pilasters and the two columns of the pronaos).

In 1754, Le Roy found one column less on the northern side and Dodwell in 1805 saw and drew three columns on the northern side (the two columns of the pronaos but only the northern pilasters).

Finally, Blouet in 1825 referred only to two columns on the northern side.

«View of Cape of Sounion».
Lithograph by A. Mayer.

EXCAVATIONS

The first limited excavations were carried out by the Dilettanti (end of the 18th century) and the Expédition de Morée under Blouet, in 1829. The first scholarly examination of the temple was carried out by the German archaeologist W. Dorpfeld in 1884 chiefly on the southern side. His accurate measurements gave us the plan of the temple and revealed the foundation of the older porous rock temple which had been destroyed by the Persians. The temple as it appeared in 1898 in fig. 1. Valerius Stais began his systematic excavation of the site in cooperation with the young architect, An. Orlando, and the subscription to the Archaeological Fund which undertook expenses. He brought many findings to light. He revealed all of the Temple of Poseidon and uncovered the Temple of Athena, thus correcting past, mistaken attributions of the temple as to which god was worshipped. Excavations of the temple and other areas in the enclosure continue to this day, carried out by the Archaeological Institute.

1. The temple before the excavation (1898).
2. The propylaea and stoes of the sacred enclosure of Poseidon during the excavations (1900).
3. The temple after the excavations (1902).

1

THE ARCHAEOLOGICAL MONUMENTS

- The Fortress of Sounio -
- The Sacred Enclosure & the Temple of Poseidon -
- The Sacred Enclosure of Athena -

THE FORTRESS OF SOUNIO

The fortress of stands on an area of approximately one acre. On the western side, towards the cape, there is a wall which, as Thucydides wrote, the Athenians built in 412 BC during the Peloponnesian War. Valerius Stais believed that the wall, built of large irregular rocks, existed before the Peloponnesian War.

The wall which Thucydides referred to began at the western end of the fortress, continued up and stopped abruptly for unknown reasons without joining the older polygonal wall.

It was built of porous rock and marble and stands in a double line. In the 3rd century BC, during the Macedonian occupation, repairs and additions were built at great expense, as the wall was strengthened with evenly cut porous rock blocks for most of its length.

The whole wall is approximately 300 metres and was reinforced at points with eleven rectangular towers. In the middle of the wall, at the point where a corner is formed, there is a tower that is larger and stronger than the others. From this point on, towards the direction of the temple, the wall is better built and has more towers. From tower number eight on, the expensive reinforcements stop. Between towers 10 and 12, there was a small gateway which was closed in the 3rd century BC when the rampart was built (7). This rampart was 170 square metres and its walls, which are 4 metres high, were built with marble blocks in a double line. Plinths were placed at the highest points, and there was a small barricade outside it.

Opinions as to the purpose of this building differ. Some claim that is was a building for purely defensive purposes; Stais, believing that it was a storage space for food or arms called it "sitovoleion" (wheat store); Svoronos believed that it was a mint while Pichard believes that it was a temple to the hero Phrontes. The last two theories can probably be safely put to rest; the one because not even a trace of metal has been found in the building and the other because the ellipsoid parvis next to the temple of Athena, has been identified as that of Phrontes.

A wall was built at the same time as the ramparts on the north west side, next to the sea. This wall is almost parallel to the existing wall built of marble blocks and has three towers. One part of the wall - the part towards the sea -touched on two small boat houses in which were two, small battle-ready vessels. In order to roll these vessels into the sea there were ramps 20.5 metres long and 11.5 metres wide on the floors which inclined towards the sea. The ramps, which had a depth of 1.25 metres,

1. Ruins of the fortress' soathouses.
2. Detail of the fortress' battlements.

1

2

had on them a wooden structure meant to protect the vessel's bottom and particularly the keel.

One entered the fortress between towers 10 and 12, passing by tower 11 and through a gate which has not survived. The path turned towards the main way, 13, of the fortress and ended up at the propylaea of the Temple of Poseidon. On the right and left of the road there were houses belonging to the municipality or to the garrison. There were also small temples (such as that of Asclepius and Apollo, Aphrodite Pontia and Zeus Meilichios who were all worshipped in the fortress). Today, a visitor enters the fortress through an opening between towers 7 and 8 and then ascends towards the temple.

From the many inscriptions that were found during excavations, we know that the Athenians sent a general and a large garrison to Sounio because they were fully aware of its strategic importance. The generals not only administered the garrison, they also ensured that the fortress had adequate supplies of food and war materiel and they supervised the repair of the walls. This is why they were frequently honoured and were offered golden wreaths. It is worth noting that that an inscription was found bearing testament to such honours and the name of the sanctuary: *"this vote to be inscribed on a stone stele and erected in the temple of Poseidon"*.

KEY TO THE TOPOGRAPHIC PLAN

1. Temple of Poseidon	7. Wheat store of the fortress
2. Southern Stoa	8. Entrance to the archaeological site
3. Entrance to the Temple	9. Polygonic wall
4. Western Stoa	10. Protective wall, end of the 5th century BC.
5. Northern Stoa	11, 12. Towers
6. Propylaea	13. Fortress' central avenue

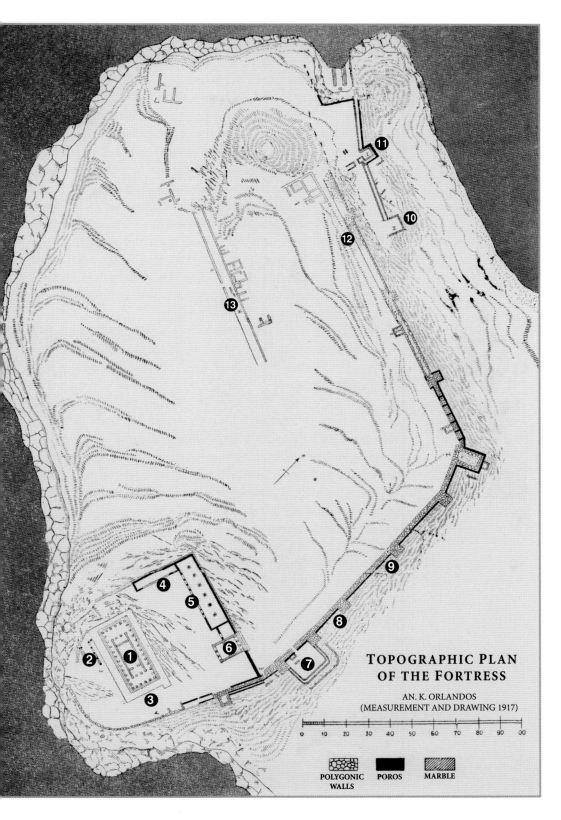

**TOPOGRAPHIC PLAN
OF THE FORTRESS**

AN. K. ORLANDOS
(MEASUREMENT AND DRAWING 1917)

0 10 20 30 40 50 60 70 80 90 00

POLYGONIC
WALLS   POROS   MARBLE

THE SACRED ENCLOSURE
AND THE TEMPLE OF POSEIDON

On the south east side of the fortress of Sounio, surrounded by a wall, there is the sacred enclosure of Poseidon. On its eastern side, a part of the wall was reinforced by the fortress wall while the rest continued the southern side of the sacred enclosure, thus forming a curve. One entered the sacred enclosure through the magnificent propylaea (which, when the marble temple was built, was covered in marble slabs to make it grander).

From both the inside and the outside there were two Doric columns which supported the pediment roof and the epistyles. In the inside of the temple, two pillars divided it along the width forming two stoes, one large and one small. The pillars with formed three doorways. The middle one, with a width of 2.2 metres, had a ramp and was used by carts, while the others (1.12 metres width) were used by those on foot.

To the right of the propylaea there was a small room which was probably used as sentry post by the garrison. Through the length of the northern side there was a stoa built of porous rock which had a length of 25 metres and a width of 9 metres. This stoa must have been built after the marble propylaea because it is supported by marble foundations and was used to protect pilgrims from bad weather and from the sun. The façade had 8 or 9 Doric columns which supported an entablature made of poros stone and on the inside there were 6 unfluted columns of poros stone which, according to V. Stais, came from the internal colonnade of the old poros stone temple of Poseidon.

A small stoa with no columns on the inside, 21 metres length by 5.5 metres width, was built later. It touched on the west side of the sacred enclosure. The temple of Poseidon, the one which has survived until these days, was built on the same foundations as the poros stone temple. Is of the Doric order, peripteral and amphiprostyle. It is peripteral because it has colonnades on each of the sides; there are 13 columns on the long and 6 columns on the narrower sides for a total of 34 columns. It is an amphiprostyle because it has two columns of the same order between the pilasters of the of the sekos (the actual sanctuary). It is built of marble which came from the quarries of Agrileza, 4 kilometres from Sounio on Laureotic Olympus.

This marble, because it contains no iron, retains its pure white colour in contrast with the Pentelic marble -of which the Parthenon was built- which has subtle yellow and gold highlights.

The temple of Poseidon and plan of the sacred enclosure.

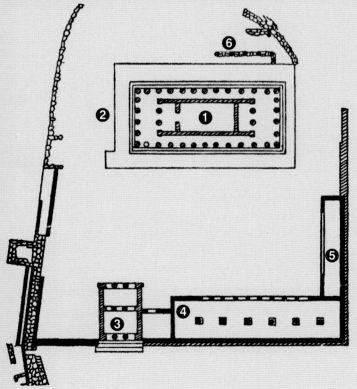

PLAN OF THE SACRED ENCLOSURE OF THE TEMPLE OF POSEIDON

1. Temple of Poseidon
2. Entrance to the Temple
3. Propylaea
4. Northern Stoa
5. Western Stoa
6. Southern Stoa

RECONSTRUCTION OF THE TEMPLE OF POSEIDON (W. PLOMMER)

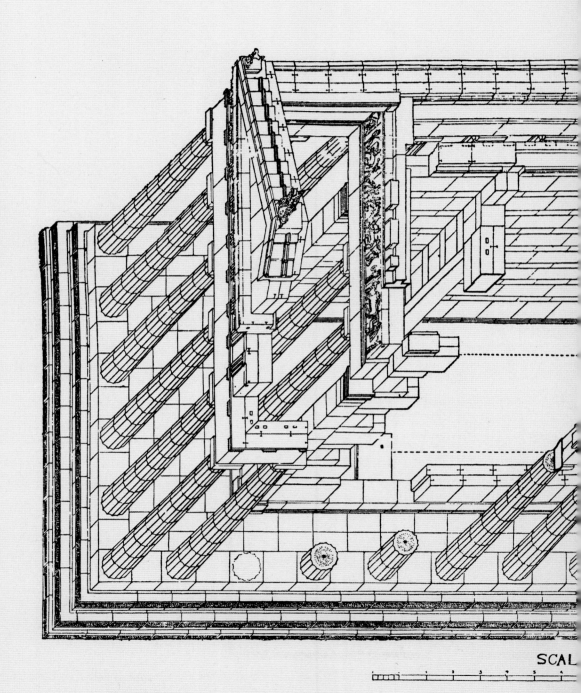

SCAL

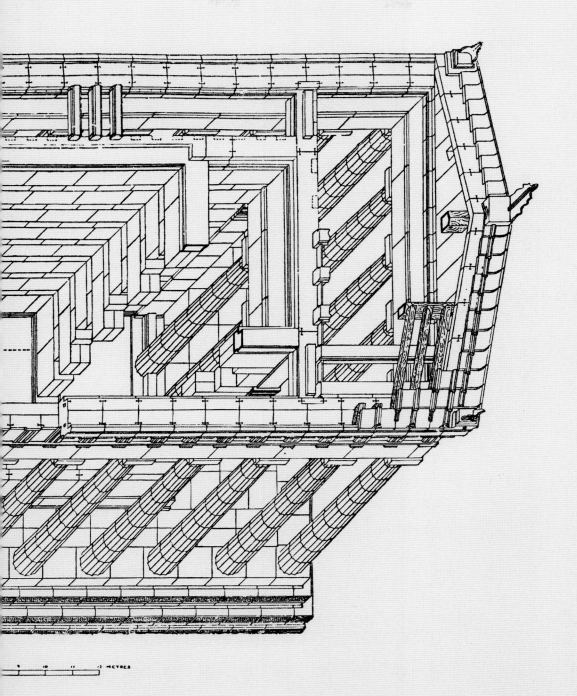

METRES

Furthermore, it is softer and more sensitive to time and to the sea salt. It is with this in mind that the architect, wanting to make his columns sturdier, reduced the fluting in the columns from the more usual 20 to 16. The columns are 6.12 metres in diameter at the base 1 and 0.79 at the highest point and they rest on a stylobate whose dimensions are 31.15 x 13.18 metres. The stylobate is the highest of the three tiers which form the base of the temple.

Opposite:
Western view of the temple.

PLAN OF THE TEMPLE OF POSEIDON (Gruben)

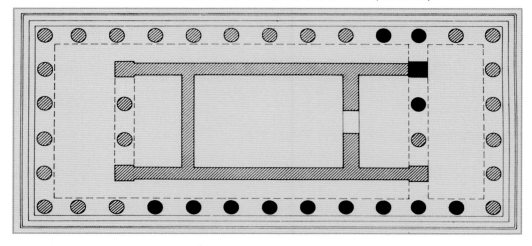

The temple and the Propylaea.

Northeast view of the temple

Northern view of the temple.

Southeast view of the temple.

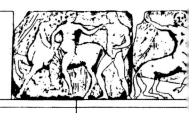

*Battle of the centaurs
from the western frieze
of the pronaos of the
Temple of Poseidon
(Delivorias).*

The temple consisted of three parts: the pronaos, the sekos, and the opisthodomos.

The pronaos and the opisthodomos had the same dimensions and each had two columns between the pilasters.

The sekos was 10.35 x 6.50 metres and there was only one access to it; through a door which lead to the pronaos.

In contrast, the opisthodomos was separated from the sekos by a wall, because this is where the precious votive offerings and the "Poseidonio money" from the mines of Laurio were kept. The statue of the god, as was customary, was in the sekos, but unfortunately, not even a trace of it has been found. Epistyles or architraves -rectangular blocks (2.52 x 0.83 metres) on which the superstructure rested - were placed on the columns. The epistyle had on it the external friezes on which the roof rested; the friezes

*The sekos
and the colonnades.*

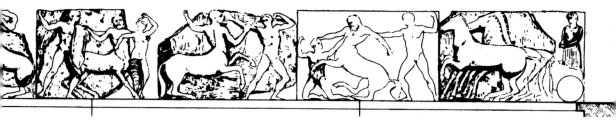

consisted of undecorated slabs alternating with triglyphs. Only four of the sides of the pronaos had decorated friezes and of these, only 14 blocks have survived. These plaques, made of Parian marble, portray scenes from the Gigantomachy (Battle of the Giants), the Centauromachy (the Battle of the Centaurs) and the labours of Theseus. The frieze of the pronaos extended to the external peristasis - something which was unusual for temples in those days. The Temple of Hephaestus, better known as the Theseion, was similar.

We know very little of the decorative work of the pediments. Archaeologists believe that the Temple of Poseidon in Sounio, the Theseion in the ancient Agora, the Temple of Ares in Acharnae and the Temple of Nemesis in Ramounta were works of the same architect whose name has not come down to us.

The eastern side and the entrance to the temple.

Countless have been the visitors to Sounio who came to admire this masterpiece of classical Greek art. Unfortunately, however, many of them, showing a woeful lack of respect to the ancient ruins, wanted to "immortalise" their names by scratching them on parts of the temple. The result of this custom - which became more popular in the last 200 years - is that the marbles have suffered the irreparable damage that we see today. Unfortunately, not even Lord Byron resisted this abominable practise; he scratched his name on the right pilaster of the temple's entry. His act was reprehensible not in that he wrote his truly glorious name, but in that he provided a bad example to others.

"Isles of Greece"
1821, Don Juan Canto III, LXXXVI, 16

Place me on Sunium's marbled steep,
Where nothing, save the waves and I,
May hear our mutual murmurs sweep;
There, swan-like, let me sing and die.

Lord Byron

THE SACRED ENCLOSURE OF ATHENA

The sacred enclosure of Athena is situated on a lower hill at a distance of five hundred metres from the sacred enclosure of Poseidon. Vitruvius, the Roman architect, was the first one to mention this temple of Athena and its peculiarities in the 1st century BC, saying: *"what is usually on the façade has been moved to the sides".* Unfortunately, he was not understood by subsequent scholars and thus the misunderstanding on the Temple of Poseidon which began with Pausanias in the 2nd century BC, continued until the 19th century.

Scyllax's account was also clear; he said: *"...Sounion is a cape and a wall; temple of Poseidon. Thoric wall and ports two..."*

We see that Scyllax did not refer to a temple of Athena, either because the Temple of Poseidon was more important, or because in his time the temple had already been destroyed.

On the northern side of the sacred enclosure there used to be an older, smaller sacred enclosure which was surrounded by large blocks.

Despite the fact that we have found nothing to help us determine who was worshipped in this large open sanctuary, N. Papahatzis and others believe that it was used to worship the hero Phrontes.

The sacred enclosure of Athena, which is certainly older than the temple of Poseidon, was surrounded by a polygonal wall made of large limestone blocks. In the inside there were two temples, one small and the other larger.

RECONSTRUCTION OF THE TEMPLE OF ATHENA
(Orlandos)

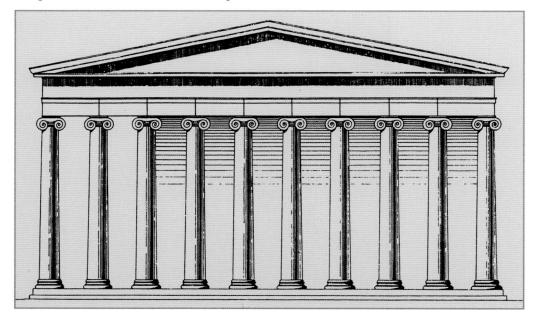

The Small Temple of the 6th century BC

The small temple was built at the beginning or in the middle of the 6th century BC. It was a simple rectangular sekos prostyle - i.e. with two Doric columns in the front that were 1.6 metres from its sides. The temple, whose dimensions are 6.8 x 5 metres, was built of unfinished blocks of stone and mud. The floor was made of a mixture of sand and lime, while the roof was wooden and the entablature was clay with engraved decorations, fragments of which have survived. The dais of the statue was found inside the temple; it had a cavity in which the plinth of the statue was placed (it seems that the statue was archaic as can be seen from the left foot).

We cannot speak with any certainty with regard to the divinity or hero to whom the temple was dedicated, although V. Stais who carried out the excavations spoke of a temple to Athena, which was subsequently replaced by a larger temple.

View of Sounio. Ruins from the sacred enclosure of Athena can be seen in the insert.

TOPOGRAPHIC PLAN OF THE SMALL TEMPLE OF ATHENA (Orlandos)

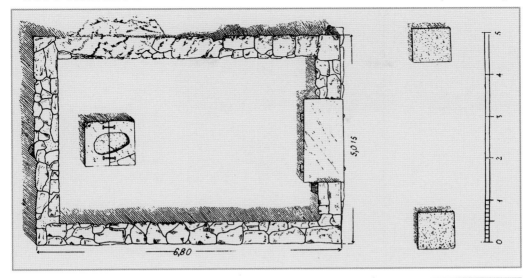

PLAN OF THE SACRED ENCLOSURE OF ATHENA

TOPOGRAPHIC PLAN OF THE SACRED ENCLOSURE OF ATHENA

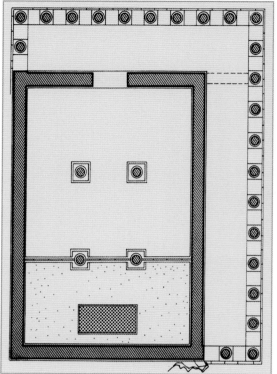

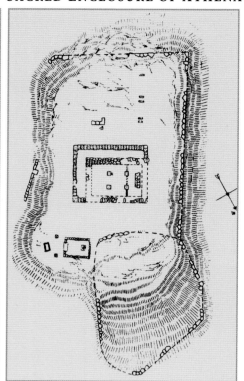

The Large Temple of Athena

The large temple, dedicated to Athena Sounias, was built of Argilezan marble as was the Temple to Poseidon. It was of the Ionic order but had many peculiarities. It had ten Ionic columns in the front side and thirteen columns on one side but not in the back. On the inside of the temple, four columns in the middle of the sekos held up the wooden roof. The floor was laid with a mixture of sand and lime while in the back there were marble floor stones on which the statue of the goddess rested. We know nothing of this statue as not even the altar has survived. The temple had a marble pediment only on its façade.

The findings from the sacred enclosure and mainly from a trench, which has a depth of 15 metres, are many and varied. The most noteworthy is the marble relief of the "Autostephanoumenos" (he who crowns himself with a wreath). Also found in this trench were a small lead kouros, the head of an archaic kore, many clay vessels, many weapons and approximately 30 clay plaques.

It is worth noting that some findings (such as the Ionic capitals of the National Museum) from the ancient Agora of Athens are thought to have come from the Temple of Athena Sounias. It is thought that this temple and some others were moved to the Agora during the reign of the Roman Emperor Augustus (31 BC - 14 BC) and reassembled.

The sacred enclosure of Athena.

ARCHAEOLOGICAL FINDINGS

FINDINGS FROM SOUNIO IN THE NATIONAL ARCHAEOLOGICAL MUSEUM OF ATHENS

Following the end of the Persian Wars, the Athenians were everywhere faced with the sight of the ruins of destroyed temples. They immediately embarked on a programme of renovations and the construction of new, more luxurious ones. The statues, the votive offerings and the sculptures which decorated the temples had been buried, as was the custom, in warehouses so as to protect them from further desecration. Thanks to their foresightedness we have been able to study archaic art in detail and this is why we have been able to study the artwork of Sounio. Many findings came to light when the trenches of the temples of Poseidon and of Athena were found.

In the sacred enclosure of Athena a funerary relief was found which represents an adolescent who is crowning himself with a wreath. The wreath with which he was crowning himself was possibly gold and was placed in holes around his hair; he is the well-known "Autostephanomenos", or "he who crowns himself". This was almost certainly not part of the temple; the relief probably came from some grave as is testified to by the shape of the plaque which must have ended in an akroterion.

There is an artificial smoothing of the marble - a characteristic of other archaic works - probably so that it could subsequently be painted. The metallic wreath must have been made of a valuable material - otherwise one cannot explain the number of holes - 11 - meant to hold it in place. The most likely story is that it represents an athlete from the trireme games which took place in Sounio in honour of Hercules. This relief is of enormous significance not only because of the originality of the subject matter, but also for its technique. The work belongs to the early days of Greek classicism. Unfortunately, the bottom part which contained the youth's legs has not survived.

Right:
The "Autostephanomenos".
Votive relief
(480 - 450 BC).

The Kouros of Sounio,
end of the 7th century BC.
Typical example of Archaic art.

Torso of a larger than life
size Kouros from approximately
600 BC and a back view
of the same statue.

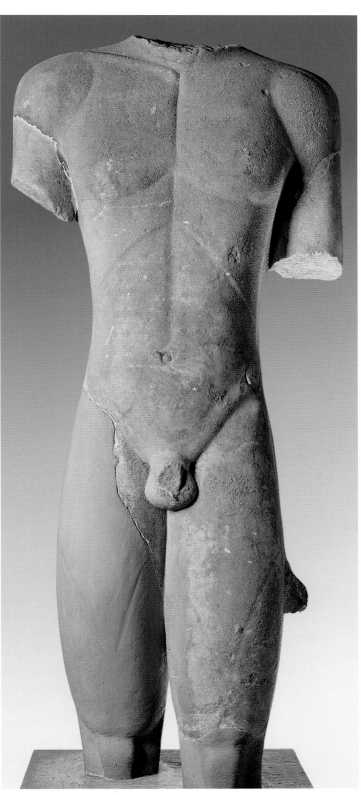

Archaic clay female busts from the sacred enclosure of Athena, 600 BC.

*Small lead Kouros
from the sacred enclosure
of Athena,
7th century BC.*

The most impressive items to have been found from the two sacred enclosures at Sounio are surely the large votive Kouroi. Each Kouros is a unique creation of the artist and of his times. All Kouroi, both votive and funerary, have common features: the nude bodies, the heavy tresses, the stiff, upright stance with fists on thighs, the slightly extended left leg, the impalpable smile.

The best preserved Kouros in the Archaeological Museum, "the Kouros of June" (no. 2720) is in room 8 of the National Archaeological Museum and has a height of 3.05 metres. Its wide shoulders and narrow waist, the protruding almond-shaped eyes with no lid, its hair, its muscles, the typical enigmatic smile, are all signs of the archaic style of this statue and they make it one of the chief works for study into the development of sculpture in Archaic times.

The stateliness of the giant body of the Kouroi, particularly their heads with the forceful expression and their imposing hairstyle, precludes any thoughts that the first Kouroi represented mere mortals, even when they were mere funerary statues.

It is worth noting that Kouroi A and B from Sounio which are in the Archaeological Museum, have nipples which look like many sided stars - a symbol of the Dioscuri. It is not a coincidence that in Attica this type of statue flourished during the period of tyranny. This period, beginning with the legislation of Dracon (624 BC) - the first legislator of the Athenian republic - until the reforms of Solon (594 BC), coincided with this type of statue, while the fall of the tyrant Hippias (510 BC) and the democratic reforms of Cleisthenes (508 BC) brought about the beginning of the end of this style.

Also noteworthy is the small lead Kouros, 8 centimetres high, which was discovered in the trench of the sacred enclosure of Athena. Despite the fact that it was made from a mold, it is a landmark in the study of such sculpture.

The head of an archaic kore, similar to those of the kores of the Acropolis made of Parian marble, was found in bad condition in the same place. It is the only marble work to have been found in the sacred enclosure of Athena which represents a kore or some female divinity. It is 11 centimetres high and has been polished in the front, while the back side, which was painted, remains rough.

A statue of a seated woman missing the head has survived from the eastern pediment of the Temple of Poseidon. As her limbs have not survived it is difficult to discern who she represents, but it is probably a nymph. The statue is 0.62 metres high and if we take into account the missing head, the height must have been 0.75 metres. Its width is 0.45 which is also the depth of the pediment.

Because the maximum height of the pediment was 1.44 metres according to Orlando's calculations, the statue must have been in the middle. With regard to the technique, the work is reminiscent of the style of Phidias which makes sense as the date of the construction of the building coincides with the period that this great artist lived.

Headless statue of a seated female figure, possibly a nymph, 730 BC.

An acroterion in the shape of a palmette made of Parian marble decorated the peak and the centre of the pediments of the Temple of Poseidon. One of these has survived in very good condition and is considered one of the best of its kind.

Fourteen pieces of the frieze depicting the Gigantomachy, the Centauromachy and the labours of Theseus from the Temple of Poseidon have survived but are in bad condition.

Of the thirty clay votive plaques that were found in the artificial trench from the sacred enclosure of Athena, only one - and indeed half of that - has survived in good condition. It has a representation of a war ship with a bearded captain at the helm and warriors with helmets and shields.

In both of the sacred enclosures many weapons, vessels, clay archaic figurines, bronze, gold and silver rings, tiny bronze tripods and small objects have been found.

1. Marble akroterion in the shape of a palmette which adorned the peaks of the pediments, approximately 400 BC.
2. Piece of a frieze from the temple of Poseidon (chariot).
3. Clay votive plague from the sacred enclosure of Athena, 7th century BC.
4. Clay vessel from the 6th century BC in the shape of a warrior wearing a helmet. Some traces of paint can be discerned. Found in the temple of Athena.
5. Corinthian aryballos with representations of animals from the sacred enclosure of Athena, 6th - 7th century BC.

4

5

LAURIO

- Modern Laurio -
- Laurio Mines -
- Ancient Agora of Laurio -
- Thorikos -

LAURIO

In the middle of the 19th century, on the orders of the Greek government, the metallurgist A. Kordellas studied the area and proved that the ancient mines could be exploited. Based on this study, the city of Laurio was created in 1864 as a gigantic metal workshop of different companies with the leading positions taken by a Greek and a French company. Mining took place for a century and was stopped in 1965. This enterprise became the first large industrial complex of Greece.

Laurio is a new city. It was established in 1864 as "Ergasteria" and was initially built around the new mining companies.

Gradually, as industry, particularly mining and metal working, developed so did the city. It had a new city plan which included the residential areas in which the metal workers and miners lived. The areas of the city have retained the names which used to indicate the descent of the workers (Italika, Roumanika, Spaniolika [Spanish], Santoriniaka etc).

The clock in Laurio Port.

There are both Orthodox and Catholic churches in Laurio. The port was moved south from Thorikos to Laurio. One can see many monuments which are characteristic of new age (1864-1987) of the mines in and around the city. A particularly impressive example is the large complex of buildings which housed the French Metal Company of Laurio. As a prime example of industrial architecture, this building has been declared a modern monument. Today, thanks to the National Technical University, it has been turned into a Technological and Cultural Park.

Another impressive building is the complex of the Greek Company. A large part has been destroyed, but some ruins of the machines which were used to wash the ores remain. The great stairs of the French Company used to load and unload cargos dominates the port. The port clock is also notable. Around the city and the port there are enormous piles of ekvolas, plinites and scoriae, leftovers from the modern mining works.

A kiln used in the mining works survives today at the port, while north east of the entrance to the city from the shore one can see traces of ancient forging works and the famous black beach with the scoriae. On entering the city from the north, one can see the Phoinikodassos (Palm Tree Forest). The city's central square is particularly interesting as there are many renovated buildings, the Fish Market and another building (Michanourgio) which today is used as a conference hall.

Laurio has rightly been called "the backdrop of the film world" as many films, documentaries and ads have been shot there.

In the last few years, following a period of rapid deindustrialisation, the city has entered a new phase of gradual, stable growth which was achieved by important changes in its economy. The port is developing into one of national significance, while the city is dynamic in the fields of commerce, services and tourism. The visitor to Laurio can find many places for entertainment or simply to have a meal.

Finally, there are two museums in the city: the Archaeological Museum (10:00– 13:00) open daily except Mondays (tel. 22920-22817) and the Mining Museum (open Wednesday, Saturday, Sunday, 10:00 – 12:00, tel. 22920-26270).

Laurio Marina (Olympic Marine s.a).
The "Galliki Skala", the bridge where ore was loaded on to ships in Laurio.

LAURIO MINES

The region of Laureotiki (Laurio, Keratea, Thorikos, Kamariza - Aghios Konstantinos, Palaea Phocea, Anavyssos) is the south east extremity of Attica which ends up in Cape Sounio. It was an area rich in ores (laura meant mine / Laurio or Lauraea area meant the place of mines) which was exploited by the Athenians and played an important role in the history of the city-state.

The exploitation of the mines must have begun around 2,800 BC when it seems that the production of silver began in Thoriko, one of the oldest inhabited areas in Attica which is next to Laurio. The mining continued during Mycenaean times (1550 - 1200 BC). The production of silver in Thoriko continued until the 7th century BC when a new era began for Laurio with the establishment of the mint. The first drachmae of Athens made of silver from Laurio were called *"eraldika"*. The next coins, the Athenian tetradrachms, were minted during the time of Peisistratus towards the end of the 6th century BC.

For the first time, coins had pictures on both sides; on the one side there was Athena and on the other there was an owl. The Athenian tetradrachmae, known as *"Laureotic glauces"* or owls, were very successful and survived in the same form even after the abolition of the tyranny.

It is worth noting that the mines were private up to the 6th century BC. By the beginning of the 5th century BC, the mines had become state owned and the demos, or government distributed revenues from the Laurio mines to the citizens. In 483 BC a rich deposit of ore was found in the Maroneia district of Laurio (near today's Kamariza) and as a result, public revenues from the mines almost doubled. The demos met to allocate more funds to the citizens.

It was at this meeting that the farsighted Themistocles, in a speech of historic significance, convinced the demos to use the

"Laurionite"
An ore whose name is linked with that of Laurio. Laurionite is an ore which was first found in the Laureotiki area. It was first discovered on the rust of metals and then later in its natural geological environment. The size of its crystals ranges from one tenth of a millimetre up to one centimetre while its colour can range from clear to a whitish grey that has the brilliance of a diamond.

"Laurionite"
Exhibit from the Laurio Mining Museum (Piet Gelaude, Piet van Kalmthout, Christian Rewitzer. Laurion: The minerals in the ancient slags, Janssen Print, 1996).

revenues to build a fleet of 200 triremes. It was with this fleet that the Athenians defeated the Persians in the Salamis straits and thus blocked the destructive passage of Xerxes.

The fifty golden years of Athenian history followed (480 - 431 BC), during which new mining and metalworking techniques were developed in Laurio. In the period from the 4th century BC to the 5th century, there was more intensive exploitation of the mines than there had been previously and this brought substantial economic gains to the city of Athens.

During this period, 20,000 slaves worked for businessmen who had their own businesses and which are today being discovered throughout the region. Among these businesses were mines, metalworking shops, huge hydraulic works for gathering water and furncaces.

According to K. Konophagos, within these two centuries, 3,500 tons of silver and 3,500,00 tons of lead were produced in the region as well as smaller quantities of iron and bronze. The production of these metals coincided with the rise of the city. Xenophon wrote: *"no matter how many workers there were, there were always enough mines and metalworking shops to absorb them"*.

This golden age for Athens and Laurio came to an end with the beginning of a most destructive war - the Peloponnesian War. In the first years of the war until 421 BC, the Spartans regularly invaded Attica and reached Laurio.

In 413 BC they conquered Deceleia, thus cutting off land communications between Athens and Euboea. The Spartans then promised the slaves their freedom and more than 20,000 slaves followed them. The silver production in Laurio thus came to an end. Work began again in the mines when Callistratus (373 - 366 BC) took over the leadership of Athens and he regulated the laws that had to do with the mines.

Laurio flourished once again for a short period, as it was indirectly harmed by the king of Macedon, Philip who, wishing to imitate the Athenians, minted his own gold and silver coins, the so-called "Philips". Philip was succeeded by his son, Alexander - known to history as Alexander the Great - who minted a new tetradrachm which had his head on the one side and the god Zeus on the other. With his conquest of the East, Alexander's coinage became very popular and eclipsed the "Laureotic glauces", bringing about a dramatic fall in the production of silver in Laurio.

Work once again began in Laurio in the 2nd century BC when Athens began again to mint silver tetradrachms. In 104 BC the

Lead plate from the Laurio mines.

slaves of Laurio rebelled and, spurred on by the slave revolts in Sicily, occupied the fortress at Sounio and plundered Attica. However, the most important reason that the mines stopped being worked seems to be that the ore was exhausted and the region was abandoned for approximately two millennia.

METALWORKS GOLD AND SILVER MINING
(Drawing by E. Smekens)

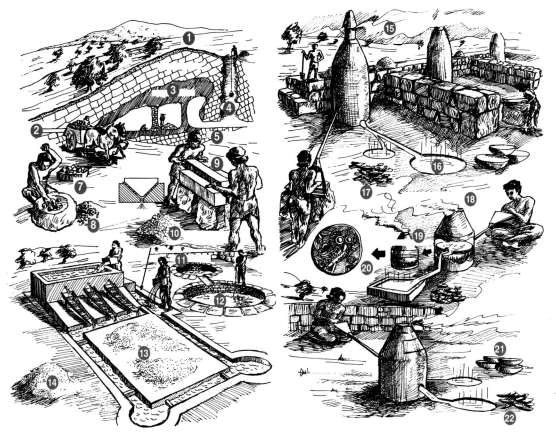

1. Mining	**7.** Crushing stone	**12.** Cistern	**17.** Scoriae
2. Galleries	**8.** Washeries-concentrating	**13.** Drying of	**18.** Furnace
3. Contact ores	**9.** Grinder	concentrated ore	**19.** Refining silver
4. Shaft	**10.** Crushed to graines	**14.** Concentrated ore	**20.** Coins
5. Limestone	<1m.m.	**15.** Furnaces	**21.** Commercial lead
6. Mechanical treatment	**11.** Settling tank	**16.** Tap hole	**22.** Scoriae

ANCIENT AGORA OF PASSA HARBOUR

The creation of a significant economic centre in the region seemed to be a natural consequence of the development of the mines; the products of the area needed to be transported and distributed. Thus, excavations brought to light the ruins of the ancient agora near the sea. A large building which has been dated to the 2nd – 1st century BC was discovered near the shore.

TOPOGRAPHICAL PLAN OF THE ANCIENT AGORA

[M. Economakou, *Archaeological Bulletin 34 (1979)130.*]

The progress of the excavations leads to the following con-clusions. The initial nucleus of the agora, i.e. the stoa at the northern side of the complex, must have been in operation during the mid 4th century BC. It is certainly older than the other parts of the agora. The rooms of the stoa were used as shops and

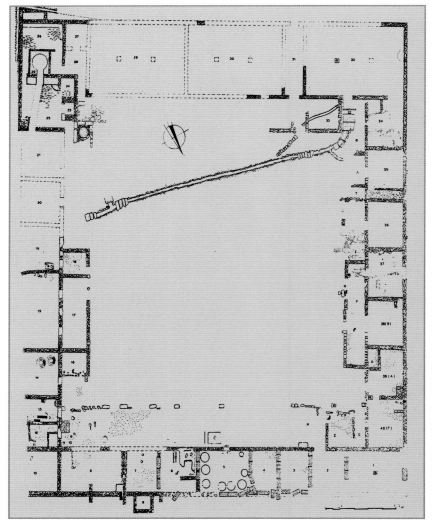

storerooms. Six large storage vessels were placed in the central room, along the length of the three walls. Also found were many broken amphorae and their lids.

As the settlement and the port developed, so did the need for the extension of the commercial centre of the region. Thus, the stoa was augmented with three additional parts and the complex became a square.

The baths were incorporated in the main building on the southern side. The exact date the addition was built is unknown. This development was, however, to have been expected as during the Hellenistic years the Agora lost its religious significance and became simply a financial centre.

THORIKOS

Thorikos is a significant archaeological site although it is not organised as one.

Modern Velatouri, a hill above the bay of Thorikos, was a Mycenaean acropolis. Thorikos was without a doubt one of the areas which benefited from the trade in metals. During the early Mycenaean period, some impressive tombs were constructed in the area. V. Stais excavated two Mycenaean tholoi there and later, Belgian archaeologists continued excavations in the area and found the foundations of many ancient houses and graves among other things.

Low on the hill, there is one of the oldest and most unusual theatres of ancient Greece. It dates back to the 6th century BC and has an elliptical shape. Left of the orchestra there was a small temple dedicated to Dionysus.

Thorikos at that time was an important financial centre which was subsequently overshadowed by Athens.

Later, the city revived to such a degree that it had its own theatre, but it was, nevertheless, rarely mentioned by the authors of antiquity. In the 4th century BC craft and workshops flourished only to decline later on and therefore contribute the decline of the whole region since then.

THE WALL BY THE SEA

The picture of Thorikos would not be complete without its sea fortifications.

There has been a limited number of excavations at this point. The plan for the wall was simple, logical and in absolute harmony with the lay of the ground. To the right, along the length of the Aghios Nikolaos peninsula, two walls were built. The first was built along the length of the lower, west hill and the second was built along the length of the slightly higher east hill (and the chapel).

On this way there was also a sort of fortress which could temporarily house –when needed- a portion of the population. A small acropolis was situated at the top of the western hill, but it was vulnerable to attacks from land.

The walls, which extend to a length of 800 metres, were fortified by the addition of at least six towers. The whole construction was complex: the walls were not intersected at any point and the towers were therefore extensions of the wall. The fortress was built by Athenians during the Peloponnesian War.

Velatouri and Mycenaean grave in Thorikos.

ANCIENT THEATRE

The theatre at Thorikos is the oldest surviving theatre in Greece. It has an ellipsoid shape – not semi-circular – as does the orchestra. At the end of the 19th century, an American team undertook the completion of the excavations and published a short report as well as a rough plan of the theatre.

The theatre has three discrete periods. The construction of the first stage dates back to the end of the 6th century BC, the second to the middle of the 5th century BC and the third to the middle of the 4th century BC. With regard to the first stage, the oldest part of the theatre is a retaining wall on which the orchestra was supported. No stone remains of the archaic theatre have been found; possibly the bare slope of the hill was used as the cavea and wooden seats were placed here and there.

In the second stage, the orchestra was enlarged following the addition of a new retaining which was at a distance of a few metres from the archaic wall and ran parallel to it. At that time, the archaic wall was sunk by the orchestra which was henceforth on a higher level. The cavea acquired 21 tiers of wooden seats, while on the west, a temple dedicated to Dionysus was built (very few fragments of this temple have survived). Two rooms were built on the east side of the orchestra.

(Unfortunately, because of the 19th century excavations, it is now difficult to discern the relationship between these rooms and the orchestra. The same applies to the arch, only the base of which survives. There is also a belief that the temple, the arch and the eastern rooms were a part of the 5th century BC construction.)

Finally, in the third stage, the cavea was greatly enlarged. A new, enormous retaining wall was built and the extra space was used to create 12 new tiers of seats, probably not of marble. The two slopes of the hill ensured direct access to the highest part of the cavea. At this period, the theatre had a capacity of 6,000 people.

The ancient theatre of Thorikos and plan of the theatre.

TOPOGRAPHICAL PLAN OF THE THORIKOS THEATRE

1. New retaining wall of the cavea.
2. Older retaining wall of the cavea.
3. Retaining wall of the orchestra.
4. Orchestra.
5. 6. Curve of the retaining wall of the cavea.
7. Temple of Dionysos.
8. Official seats. 9. Altar.
10. 11. Ramps leading to the cavea.
12. 13. Chamber carved from surrounding rock.

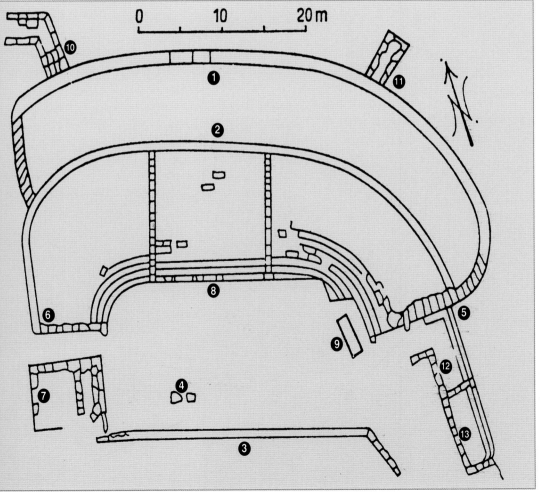

Above: Reconstruction of a sacrifice at Sounio.

Below: Photograph from the unique Manos Hatzidakis concert next to the Temple of Poseido.

GLOSSARY

Akroterion: Strictly, a pedestal at the corners or peak of a roof to support an ornament and more usually the ornament itself.

Amphiprostyle: Marked by columns in porticoes only at the front and back (of a classical temple), not on the sides.

Entablature: In classical architecture, the elaborated beam member carried by the columns, horizontally divided into architrave (below), frieze and cornice (above). The proportions and detailing are dilerent for each order, and strictly prescribed.

Epistyle: The main beam or architrave laid horizontally over the capitals of a column, from one to the next, to form a continuous bed for a superstructure to rest on.

Frieze: The middle horizontal member of a classical entablature, above the architrave and below the cornice, or a similar decorative band in a stringcourse, or near the top of an interior wall below the cornice.

Opisthodomos: The inner portico at the rear of the sanctuary of a classical temple, corresponding to the pronaos in the front.

Palmette: A column capital or decoration resembling the leaves of a palm tree.

Pediment: In classical architecture, the triangular gable end of the roof above the horizontal cornice, often llled with sculpture.

Peripteral: A building surrounded by a single row of columns.

Pronaos: The inner portico in front of the naos, or sanctuary, of a classical temple.

Propylaea: (pl) The monumental gateway to a sacred enclosure.

Sacred enclosure: A sacred site for the worship of a god or hero.

Sekos: Cella or innermost sanctuary of a temple.

Stylobate: Strictly, the single top course of the three steps of the base upon which the columns rest directly.

Triglyph: The characteristic ornament of the Doric frieze, consisting of slightly raised blocks of three vertical bands separated by V-shaped grooves. The triglyphs alternate with plain or sculptured panels called metopes.

Votive: A sacred propitiatory olering to a god.

Note: The delnitions in the glossary were provided based on "The Illustrated Dictionary of Historic Architecture", edited by Cyril M. Harris, Dover Press, Toronto, 1977.

« The last sounds of Greece»

...Our sailors had everything in readiness to sail. We sailed out into the open
sea and the breeze blowing from the shore pushed us briskly to Tzia.
The further we went, the more beautiful seemed the columns of Sounio on the
waves. I saw them clearly outlined in the blue sky because they were pure white
and the evening was a pure blue. We were quickly distanced from the cape, but
in our ears the waves crashing on the rocks still rang as did the murmur of the
air in the bushes and the song of the cicadas which are today the only
inhabitants of the ruins of the temple.

Francois August René Chateaubriand
"Journey: The Greece of 1806"

«On aspalathoi»

Sounion was lovely that spring day
the feast of the Annunciation.
Sparse green leaves around rust-coloured stone,
red earth, and aspalathoi
with their huge thorns and their yellow flowers
already out.
In the distance the ancient columns, strings
of a harp still vibrating….
Peace. - What could have made me think
of Ardiaios?
Possibly a word in Plato, buried in the mind's
furrows: the name of the yellow bush
hasn't changed since his time.

That evening I found the passage:
"They bound him hand and foot," it says,
"they flung him down and flayed him,
they dragged him along
gashing his flesh on the thorny aspalathoi,
and they went and threw him into Tartarus,
torn to shreds."
In this way Aridiaios, the terrible Pamphylian
tyrant,
Paid for his crimes in the nether world.

Complete Poems of Giorgos Seferis
Translated by Edmund Keeley
and Philip Sherrard
Anvil Press, pg. 223
"The last sounds of Greece"

BIBLIOGRAPHY

- STAIS, VALERIUS, *Ανασκαφή εν Σουνίω*. Archaeological Bulletin (1900, 1917). *Το Σούνιο και οι ναοί Ποσειδώνος και Αθηνάς* (1920).
- ORLANDOS, K., *Το αέτωμα του εν Σουνίω ναού του Ποσειδώνος*. Archaeological Bulletin (1915). *Του εν Σουνίω ναού του Ποσειδώνος τοίχος και οροφή*. Archaeological Bulletin (1917). *Η γραπτή αρχιτεκτονική διακόσμησις του εν Σουνίω ναού του Ποσειδώνος*. Archaeological Bulletin (1953 – 1954).
- IATROU, G., *Σούνιο-Λαύριο, Κερατέα* (2003)
- KAROUZOU, S., *Εθνικό Αρχαιολογικό Μουσείο, Συλλογή Γλυπτών*. Athens, 1967.

- DINSMOOR, W. B., *The Temple of Ares at Athens*, Hesperia, IX (1940)
- DINSMOOR, W. B. Jr., *The Temple of Poseidon*. American Journal of Archaeology, 78 (1974).
- KENNY E.J.A, *The Ancient Docks on the Promontory of Sounion*. British School Annual, XLII (1947)
- PLOMMER, W. H., *Three Attic Temples,* British School Annual, XLV (1950) - *The Temple of Poseidon on Cape Sounion: Some Further Questions*. British School Annual, 55 (1960).

Texts: GEORGIOS TERLAKIS
Text editor: DAPHNE CHRISTOU
Translation: TANIA KANTZIOS
Artistic editor: EVI DAMIRI

Production - Printing: M. Toubis S.A..

We would like to thank Mr. Stavros Iatrou for his contribution to this book.
(Texts on the metal works and modern Laurio).